AUG. 2000

UNBRIDLED

TO JANE & BILL, DEAR
OLD FRIENDS.
ENJOY MY BOOK!,

Susan Cunningham

No part of this book may be reproduced in any form or by any electronic or mechanical means including photocopying or recording without permission in writing from the publisher, except by a review to quote brief passages in a review. For information, consult publisher, Bravado Publishing Ltd., P.O. Box 976, Skaneateles, NY 13152 (315) 472-5814.

Printed and bound in the United States of America.

Library of Congress Catalogue Number: 99-94386

ISBN 0-9671551-0-X

FOR MY TWO BEST FRIENDS

Fran, my love, my hero
and
Sewz who never objected
to sharing me with Fran

ACKNOWLEDGMENT

I've been overwhelmed with Diana's remarkable capabilities, her tireless efforts and dogged determination that has put this book in your hands. Now I'm overwhelmed with gratitude. Thank you D!

AUTHOR'S NOTE

I was always told to "think like a horse", to better understand them and improve my riding skills. I found myself "thinking like a horse" all the time, even when I wasn't in the saddle. You could always see their moods and know what they were saying. More often than not, their tales would fall into rhyme and I'd quickly write them down before I'd forget. A cat or a dog will talk to you with a bark or a meow, but a horse's silent voice is just as loud and clear.

So here are some of their thoughts and tales. They are in a different typeface as they are talking their own language, "horse sense".

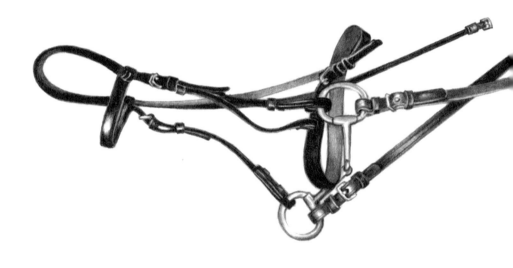

UNBRIDLED
HORSE THOUGHTS AND TALES

Written and Illustrated

by

Juann Cunningham

BRAVADO PUBLISHING LTD.

Syracuse, New York

When I was a little girl, I was hypnotized by a horse, to forever be under their spell.

We lived in a small town where you didn't see horses every day. I'm sure it was that little grey and white pony. The man brought him around every spring to have your picture taken on his back for proud parents and grandparents. But no one was prouder than I. That picture stood on my bureau for years, and every night I'd kiss the glass before I went to bed, as though he were mine.

His name was "Mousey," not my choice, but it was tooled on the leather of his western stirrups. I wore my mother's grey suede boots that were hers as a child and I remember how delighted I was when they finally, really fit me. From then on, I drew pictures of horses. I wrote poems about horses. I dreamed of horses. I was totally hooked, and I guess I'm still that same little girl.

In those days, we had a milkman. He came by dark of night, usually about 2 a.m., and occasionally I'd hear the clip-clop of his horse's hooves on the pavement in front of our house. I'd get up and rush to the window. I'd hear the rattle of the bottles as he made his delivery, and then the clip-clop again.

At that moment, I could catch a glimpse of them passing under the street light, he and his horse. I knew they knew each other well and yearned for that kind of a relationship with my very own horse.

My parents had a friend who had his very own horse in the next town. When they mentioned going to visit him, I could hardly wait for the day to come.

The horse was a huge thoroughbred named Sugar. He was a foxhunter the color of a copper penny. He was magnificent! He blocked the sun when I looked up at him, and my heart leaped when the man put his arm down to pull me up on the saddle in front of him. He told me to hold the mane with both hands and we started to move: The beginning of the ride that would take me many miles and most of a lifetime of wonderful memories.

I hounded my parents to let me take lessons at school. It was a banner day when they finally agreed. It wasn't my own horse, but I was working my way up to it and I could certainly make believe!

The instructor's son picked us up in an old woody station wagon, eight silly girls in their ill-fitting riding outfits. We sang and giggled and screamed, wound up with excitement on our way, until he had to beg us to quiet down every time.

Coming home was another story, mostly talk of the lesson, and much quieter songs. Some of us fell asleep. You see, we were all dreaming of the same thing.

We took lessons for several years and showed locally a bit, one school against the other. I won some ribbons, but I'm sure it wasn't for any ability of my own, only the horse. I must have looked cute with my little pigtails and always smiling.(I still smile all the time when I'm on a horse because no one could be having as much fun as I!) I'm convinced the judges loved it. However, we were never allowed to brush a horse or clean a hoof or braid a mane or care for them in any way. The horse was brought to us cleaned, brushed and tacked up and we rode into the ring on a push button horse. Something was really missing and I needed the missing ingredient.

As we grew and became young ladies we went our separate ways. We'd ride together on holidays when we could, and finally most of us left the group and married.

Only a war stopped me from being involved with horses. When I sent a picture to my husband overseas of our first born on a horse with me at six weeks old, the return letter made me realize I had been thoughtless, to say the least. He didn't need anything else to worry about. They were shooting real bullets at him over there. I packed away a few of my dreams for the moment and got my priorities straight.

I played house and raised kids for twenty-one years. Amazingly didn't miss the horses at all. But suddenly everyone was all grown up, my husband traveled a lot and my lap was really empty.

About that time a friend happened to drop in on her way from her riding lesson, and she smelled sooooo good! The hypnosis was beginning to activate. She asked if I rode. I told her my story and suddenly I said yes to taking a lesson with her. How far could I fall? How far could he run? It was in an arena.

When I walked into the barn, there was something so timeless about that moment. The smells, the sounds, I even recognized all the old horses, though it had been long ago and far away and they couldn't have been the same. I still knew them all anyway. I was entranced and I was that little girl again.

My first new equine friend was a lesson horse named Seymour. He looked like a Ubangi warrior when he was snoozing, his bottom lip hung so low. He wasn't a handsome fellow, but he had a heart of pure gold. He was trustworthy and patient and no matter who was on his back, he did what was asked of him. He was a "learning machine", an honest soul who taught everyone to ride. We used to say he would do his yoga while circling the ring with his lessons. You could almost hear him hum. When he would be leased for a foxhunt he was equally priceless, but you had to jiggle his bit, tap him three times with your crop, and say, "Hey, Seymour, it's me, wake up, we're in for some fun!" and he'd be fabulous. Well, the first tale is his, and I know he's speaking for all lesson horses everywhere. They are the best!

The Lesson Horse (for Seymour)

When you want to graze and the day is hot
And they don't care if its hot or not
So they take you out for a little trot,
It's tough to be a horse!

The little kids just want to run.
The temperature is 91.
Do they really think that this is fun?
It's tough to be a horse!

The haughty woman, all too fat,
With the riding whip and the derby hat,
Thinks she can ride if she's dressed like that,
Her whip's the driving force!
She thinks she's light to lug around.
Her hands are heavy and her bottom pounds.
I'd like to dump her on the ground.
It's tough to be a horse!

The skinny man with legs of steel,
Who'd buy me if he'd get a deal,
Could kill me with those iron heels!
He'll show me who's the boss!
They lease my body for a fee.
He wants his money's worth, you see.
Well next time he can carry me!
It's tough to be a horse.

When the day is through and your back is sore
And you've lugged eight lessons, what a bore,
    And they tell you that there's just one more
You smile and say , "Of course!"
But it's tough to be a horse!

Our instructor was a fabulous man who knew how to bring out the best in the horse and the rider. His keyword was fun. He was Master of the Foxhounds, President of the polo club and the Horse Council, but nothing gave him more delight than to involve a newcomer in his addiction. At this point, I was the target. He was the pied piper and we all danced to his music. There was never any doubt in my mind that I could do whatever he asked in our lessons. I counted the days each week until Tuesday night.

One night, his wife called to tell me he'd be a little late, he was tied up at JFK. I lied when I said, "Oh, he's been on a trip? I don't mind canceling." She responded, "No, no, he'll just be a half hour late." I was smiling again.

When he arrived at the barn, he was in a business suit, eating a sandwich. He had just flown in from Dusseldorf, Germany to give little ole' me a ten dollar lesson. I was flattered beyond belief and so impressed!

He was a fountain of knowledge and information. We dwelled on every word. He would entertain us with his wonderful horse stories, every one hilarious!

The lessons were never limited to an hour. We were having so much fun we'd all forget the time, except, that is, for my twenty-five year old lesson horse. As we were all standing around one night, still mounted and drinking in all the stories, he was falling asleep and decided to lie down! Everyone yelled and I caught him just in time! Dave laughingly said he'd have to make his stories more interesting for the horses.

At this point, I realized riding once a week was not going to be enough and I started to save my hem and buttonhole money from my little sewing business. By the end of the year I was ready!

I asked Dave if he would find a horse for me. He knew best. The horse had to be solid color (more about that later), old enough to know better, young enough to last as long as I would, and I didn't want an impersonal drone. I had to have a real friend who responded to me above all others.

Shortly thereafter I was told a horse had been found for me and I was introduced to a lovely four year old mahogany bay gelding. He was a Morgan-Standardbred cross, an incongruous combination. His big innocent eyes and "little boy lost" expression sold me immediately. When I rode him, he felt comfortable and did everything willingly. I felt he was aiming to please even though he was just a little "greenie."

My husband, Fran, insisted I think about my decision a few days. He has far more common sense than I do and I tend to be a little impulsive. I had looked at no other horses. How could the first one be the right one?

Well, maybe because Dave picked him for me.

Unbeknownst to me, the owner brought him over to the barn for me to use for the week. When he called three days later and asked if I had been enjoying him, I raced to the barn. The little guy was anxious to get out of his stall after a three day lockup, and I thought it best to turn him loose in the arena. He flew into the arena as I climbed on a four foot ledge that circled the walls, for a good vantage point. No salesman ever made such a pitch! No huckster ever showed his product so well! He rolled, leaped, twisted and squealed with delight, then raced and bucked and rolled again. When the energy was expended, he quietly trotted over to me and, honor bright, put his big head in my lap... he sure filled that empty space, literally. I guess you could say that he picked me, too. We had found each other.

I made an immediate telephone call, and he was mine! We've been together over twenty years now and this is his tale of our partnership in the beginning, and over the years.

Trusting Partners (for Sew 'n Sew)

I trust her and she trusts me
That's just the way it has to be!
There was a time when we were new,
I didn't know just what to do.
I'd question many things she'd say.
I liked to do it all my way.

I didn't like to be restrained.
I'd rather run and not be trained.
I'd spook at anything we passed
And everything I did, was <u>fast</u>!
After all, how did she know
What was "safe" where 'ere we'd go?

I used to always be alarmed
If she would take me from the barn,
And try to run home all the way
Lest someone else should get my hay,

But it was funny how she knew
'Twas always there when we were through.

She taught me that it wasn't wise
To shy at baby butterflies.
I'm so big and they're so small,
They really couldn't hurt at all.
What she asked was not too wrong,
So it seemed okay to play along.

We learned to jump when I was ready.
I crossed a thousand cavellettis.
If I'd get nervous, she would say
"Don't worry, Buddy, it's okay!"
And sure enough I'd do just fine;
'Twas as if she knew it all the time.

The jumps got up to quite a height,
But she made me want to do it right.
She'd give my sides a little squeeze,
Say "You can do it!" with her knees.
I didn't have to rush a fence
Somehow what she said made sense!

I don't know how she got so smart.
I'd never guessed it at the start.
But she has shown the two of us
Can do it all with little fuss.
She listens to me more and more.
I guess she sees, I know the score!

When there's a rifle in the woods,
I let her know it isn't good.
She calls the old dog and we go
The other way 'cause I say so.
Now you know, its very plain to see,
She trusts me now implicitly!

When we chase the fox, it's my domain!
She rides me with an easy rein.
She sets me in my proper place
And lets me know its not a race!
Then leaves the rest to me alone
And knows I'll get us safely home.

She views each season of the year
Upon my back, she need not fear.
I take her safely over ditches
And in return she'll scratch my itches.
Being partners can be fun,
When she's up top, we think as one!

Now, all the while she's been assumin'
The horse's thoughts and I the human's.
And so we've come to each depend
On one another as a friend.
We suit each other to the letter
I couldn't have it any better!

...and neither could I. He is my dear friend.

In moving into Dave's polo barn, we became one of a dozen lucky boarders to spend the next several years together, sort of an extended family.

We were all adults, but all of the youngsters who took lessons and worked at the barn could show us a thing or two and we all took advantage of their expertise. Age differences melted away. We were a family and there was always someone to ride with.

We had work days with picnic lunches, built jumps and cleared trails for the hunts then had the fun of trying them first. Never worked so hard or had so much fun... good food... good company... great times.

Saturdays were the busiest, all the lessons, from beginners to the adults...the little ones' lesson was after ours and they'd be waiting for us to finish, all in a row. I could see myself in their faces...so long ago.

Our winters are pretty bad in central New York and though I would go outside right up until it was downright impossible, when the snow reached our girth, we were finally forced to ride inside.

Sundays all the boarders would ride in the arena with Dave usually doing a little "stick and balling" down at the end. When everyone was there and all doing their own thing, we began to need a little traffic control. Dave took over and got us in line. Before we knew it, we were doing figure 8's, pairs and circles, just like the Mounties! It was a great way to spend a Sunday afternoon.

It wasn't a surprise when Dave's innovative mind came up with the idea to organize a drill team for the ladies. You had to be over sixteen (didn't want a pony club look) and have a solid color brown or black horse between 15 and 16.2 hands who would get along with other horses. Generally, the horses liked it as much as the humans and quickly learned the patterns. It was great training for young horses as well as the ladies. There was a scramble to get the right color horse to be on the team. The men who were boarders kindly loaned us their horses. For the ladies who had greys or apps or palominos, Dave was kind enough to fill our numbers with some of his polo ponies and would pick up our members spread around the countryside with his big rig for practices and performances.

Some of our members were sort of standing on the fringe, anxious to get involved but didn't have a horse. Our daughter was one of them. She jumped at the chance to take over the care of a beautiful, young, chestnut, thoroughbred mare from a benevolent boarder who just didn't have time for her.

Fleety Sal had a difficult childhood, going from one "foster care" to another. Anyone who saw her when our daughter was with her would say, "I remember that horse, I trained her!" Well, how many trainers can you have had when you're only a four year old? She always belonged to the same family and was trying to do what they all wanted.

She was a sweet mare, not a mean bone in her body. She wasn't a kicker or a biter, but she did demand her own space and made that perfectly clear to the other horses during the eighteen years she was with us. Her ears went back and she'd turn her back if she disapproved of someone, and would "snake" the little one if he came too close.

Her instincts were first rate and when they came into play, all was lost.

At this point, I must insert a little story about dear Miss Sally. My daughter and I were riding one day and Sally suddenly became obsessed with a fly on her belly! She kept kicking at it and biting at it. My daughter stroked the crop back and forth underneath her, but nothing would remove the pest! Finally, we decided just to take off and the wind would blow it loose.

From a flat gallop, Sally suddenly dropped straight to the ground, frantically rubbing her belly side to side like a dog with a relentless flea. Then, she leaped to her feet and continued at the same pace! Our astonished daughter, having amazingly stayed seated all the while, shook her head in disbelief. When Sally wanted to do something, it didn't matter if you were on her back or not. After all, she did have a bad itch!

She would panic when she found herself alone. She would flirt with every stranger and there would be no containing her. I'm convinced she would have been a fine broodmare, but she missed her greatest calling and was never bred. I think this was a real loss, as she was such a beauty. If I hadn't learned to love her, and I was less than kind, I would say she was an airhead, but it would be nicer to say she was totally confused. This is her tale.

I'm Trying (for Fleety Sal)

Isn't it enough that I'm strikingly
Beautiful and all heads turn when I pass?
It's difficult for me to clutter my mind
With these trivial things that she asks!

They say that my brain is the size of a pea.
Just how much does she think I can store in it?
I get rattled and flustered with new information.

I don't think I can get any more in it!
But I'm trying....

I know that she knows that I'm trying
To please, but really is all this a necessity?
I never could get this changing lead thing,
It creates so very much stress in me.

I'm so lovely and grand as I run through the
Fields, but there's only one move that will slow me.
If the horse that is following turns out of
Sight, his departure so suddenly will whoa me!

When she's cleaning my hooves and she's
On the near side and she asks for the hoof that she wants,
I jiggle around and I give her the far one,
After all, its the effort that counts!
'Cause I'm trying....

Backing up is something I can't figure
Out, yet she constantly asks me to do it.
Over fences I always cut out to the left,
After, before, or into it!

She says that we both have a chronic
Death wish and that's why we're such birds of a feather.
I don't know what she wants! She won't
Listen to me!...so we'll probably go down together!

To know she's become my very best friend
Is so wonderfully gratifying.
And in speaking of me to the man at the
Barn, she said I was really trying.
That I'm very, very trying...

Sally faired well on the team, but for the little incident

in the box pattern when she felt the need to attempt to jump over another horse who was simply in her way.

The drill team was a huge success for fun and glory. Dave was a real stickler for perfection, and would tell us we were "out of uniform" if we wore different cufflinks, but in fact, his eye for detail is what made us look so good. It was most important that each horse and rider look exactly like the others and we used to say, jokingly, "if anyone falls off, everyone falls off. Make it look like part of the act. If you break a leg, we'll paint the cast black, like a boot, and you'll perform anyway."

When Dave finally worked out the finished ride, he asked us to memorize it and then just put it away and not share it with anyone not on the team. We all swore we'd do that, then chew it up and swallow it. No spy would ever lay eyes on it.

After months of practices, meetings and total commitment, we were ready! Wearing blue and white uniforms with matching accessories on the horses, twenty-four ladies were ushered onto the field by two ladies on greys carrying the American flag and the team flag.

As the music began, my horse would grow taller, standing at attention. I could feel his heart beating against my knees. He knew what he had to do. He was in charge and it was up to him to make sure everything went right. You see, he had memorized the ride, too. We felt we were even better than the Mounties because we did all the patterns with jumping as well and, besides, we were prettier. The applause at the finale was intoxicating. We were all on a high for weeks because the compliments kept on coming.

We performed at local shows, field days, fund raisers at the polo games, even race tracks and the State Fair. Dave's enthusiasm and pride kept us going for several years.

The men couldn't stand us having all the fun and when it was announced that there would be a polo clinic at the barn, everyone signed up, including some of the ladies.

It was arranged to rent horses from Cornell University for the summer for everyone's first year of polo. You have to understand that these horses had all been donated to Cornell and were a variety of breeds and backgrounds and your name went into a hat for each practice. Sometimes you'd get a runaway, a slow poke you couldn't move, an old hunter, a show horse or a reiner.

Everyone was given a mallet and ball and the fun began, the reins in one hand and mallet in the other. Poor Seymour, who had been dragged into the clinic so everyone would have a horse, just wouldn't move. It wasn't a lesson. What were we doing here? The girl on his back was paddling his sides so hard to get to the ball she looked like a canoer desperately trying to avoid the waterfall. Actually, the ball could be found underneath her. Then we had the show horse who had never been out on a polo field who figured he'd better leave this crazy place in a hurry, especially when this nut on his back was waving a big stick around his head. He was off the field and down the road in moments, and it was a real chore to get him back, I might say.

Some of the horses who had done some polo before had such good brakes the novice riders didn't expect the obedient stops. We called the result an emergency terrain check.

It was a comedy of errors. The only ones missing were Curly, Moe and Larry. But they could only get better, and they did — better and better. They all survived the beginnings and by midsummer, everyone had accepted the mallet and the sound of it on the ball...no small task, I might say, but Dave made everything seem easy. "Of course you can, anyone can do it," he would say.

When they paraded out on the field in their polo whites and full regalia to play a seven minute chukker in their first Sunday game, Prince Charles really had nothing on them and the polo stories have been going on ever since!

Polo was king that summer. I always thought it was a most difficult game for a horse to understand, but I've been told that many horses learn to love it and actually follow the ball.

This tale is for all of them, but especially speaking for Paul Lowery, an old friend who played a great game for so many years.

The Polo Pony (for Paul Lowery)

There's a game we play in summer when
The temperature is high and the grass is
Sweet and luscious as can be;
On a field that's chewed down close, with
Seven other guys, and their masters and
My master and me...

Now the object of the game, you see, is to
See who sweats the most and each one
Gets a turn to try his best;
And to make it more amusing for the men
Upon our backs, they play a game called "polo"
with the rest.

They each carry a stick, which I didn't
Like a bit, but I got used to it as time
Did pass,
And they all run around and chase a
Ball that's on the ground, while they seem
To kill some snakes upon the grass!

We go in one direction, then he wants
Me in another, I can't seem to please
Whatever way I go.
But soon I realized that all the

Racing and gyrations are designed
To make the perspiration flow!

Now it seems to give them pleasure if they
Hit the ball a distance, especially if it goes
Between the posts.
I guess it takes some skill to keep it from
The others, and if they do, they get a
Chance to boast!

Well, a week ago last Sunday, we were
In a super match and the score was close
And all were in high gear.
I was pretty lathered up, and knew I had a chance
To win, but seven others had the same idea!

We were running down the field and the
Ball was dead ahead when this big bay
Barrels by me with a grin...
It seemed just like a race, but I didn't
Like his face, and you could bet your
Bucks I wouldn't let him win!

Now I'm just a little guy, but I knew that
I could beat him, and my boss gave me
The cue to go ahead.
We were at his side in seconds and I
Gave him such a shove, that he quickly
Saw — the ball was ours instead!

My master reined me in and turned me
On a dime; with his stick he gave the
Ball a mighty wallop!
He hit it once again and left the others
In our dust because there's no one that
Can catch us at a gallop!

The ball sailed through the posts and

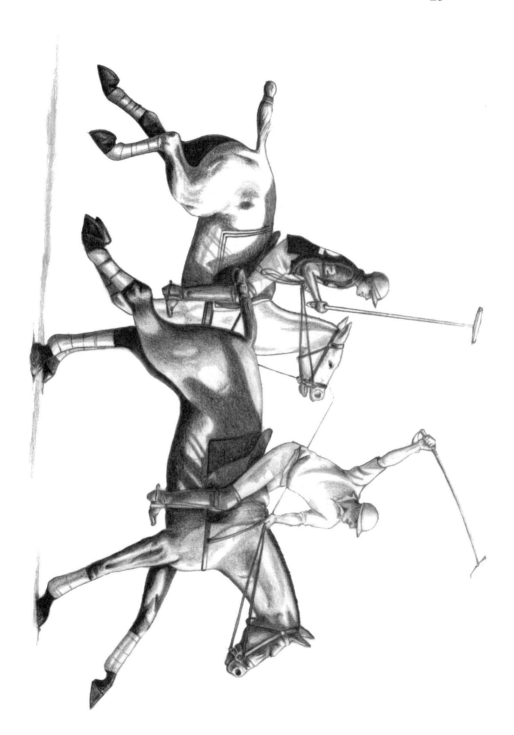

The crowd let out a roar, horns were
Honking and I knew that we had won!
With the perspiration pouring and the happy
Crowd still roaring, I surely was
One proud son of a gun!!

I was hot and I was tired but I
Knew that we'd played well, when we left the field
He gave my neck a pat.
What it takes to play this game is a strong
And healthy frame and a guy who under-
Stands you on your back!

Later from the grandstand, I heard them call
My name and my boss and I
Walked forward, filled with pride!
Then a pretty lady kissed me and they gave me
A new cooler that said, "Best Playing Pony"
On its side!

In my stall that evening, I could hear them
Celebrating...The champagne toasts were
For me and I knew it.
It showed me if there's anything in life
You want to go for
It sure pays to put your heart and sweat
Into it!

I never did get involved with playing polo. I felt Sewz
and I had too much to learn about each other the first year or so.
He was still too green and so was I. I didn't want to have the
team depending on us if we couldn't come through for them.
Besides, he really hated the crack of the mallet!

We did love to trail ride and we never missed a day, rain,
shine, sleet or gloom. We'd do about six to eight miles a day. He

was so fit he looked like a greyhound. We got the reputation of knowing every trail in a five mile radius.

We loved company, but my hectic daily schedule didn't afford the luxury of many pre-arranged dates so we'd ride alone if no one was at the barn ready to join me. We live on the outskirts of a small town surrounded by dairy farms interspersed with residential areas. We ride the back roads and farm roads into the fields and woods.

We've learned to deal with bicycles, motorcycles, roller bladers, tractors, trucks trailing boats, attacking dogs, combines (that was a sticky wicket!), huge milk trucks from the dairy farms (not the old wagon delivery of yore) and snow plows.

One time I really had a scary problem. We were out alone on a lovely day in the fall and I was following the route that the hunt had taken the day before. It brought us the length of a hay field to a hedgerow where there was a painted stone coop. I thought it would be a good experience for him to take it outdoors. He never liked that stone coop in the arena. They all looked so much bigger indoors.

He took the jump without hesitation, but on the other side a tractor road bordered the hedgerow and as we landed and started to the left we found ourselves ensnared with all fours in a great, loose bundle of baling wire! It was like landing in a big slinky!

Sewz panicked. The more he flailed around to get out of it, the more entangled he became! It obviously wasn't something we could just run away from. I was so afraid he'd tear his legs to pieces. There was nothing to do but get off. I said a prayer he'd trust me enough to stand still and let me get him out of this. He was really terrified. Every time he moved, the wire would spring up and coil in another direction. He must have thought it was alive and out to get him! When I tried to move it away from him, the same thing happened! I talked and cooed to him and told him he had to be very brave and he was my very best, favorite horse and he finally stood still, I think in desperation. He was shaking with fright and wanted to run. I had to stand on the wire as I removed it from each leg... one at a time, keeping it from springing again. It seemed like an hour, but it probably took about five minutes in all, one of the longest five minutes in my life.

He was so happy to be free and unencumbered again when I got back on. He bucked with happiness half the length of the hay field on the way back. I think that experience made him realize we were in all this together and he could depend on me, and I on him.

I went back later to remove the wire. It must have fallen off one of the farm wagons, the farmer never knowing he lost it or what could have happened that day, or, even worse, if it fell off his wagon the day before when many more riders could have taken the same jump, one after the other.

Dave taught hunt seat for our lessons and with his being Master of the Foxhounds, the ultimate goal was for us to join him in his field. Six of us would be the new hunters from his barn that year.

It wasn't wise for a new rider to take a green horse. Everyone wanted Seymour. He had been vaguely promised to four different people, me being one of them. In my heart I wanted Sewz and I to go together, but a first time horse, first time rider seemed like asking for problems. On the other hand, I had ridden him every single day since I bought him the year before and we sure were getting to be partners.

Dave called for a mock hunt to check us all out. He wanted to be proud of his group in the company of ten guests joining us from other barns. He had been teaching us the etiquette of the hunt for a few years so we had an edge on the others, but happily sat through the slide show with Dave's humorous commentary. If you want to start foxhunting, even if you've shown for ten years, it's a whole new ball game. Trail ride for a year with lots of company and tell everyone to bring their dog! It will make it easier for both you and your horse. Then, take a clinic.

We set out on the trail after lunch.

The horses immediately got into the spirit of the thing. They loved to be doing things with other horses instead of another solo performance. A few horses became overzealous and we had a couple of runaways. One young lady soon discovered the Master wasn't pleased to be shown her horse was faster than his. That's a real no no! As for myself, I found early on the origin of the phrase "here's mud in your eye." If mud in your eye means good luck, I was covered with luck by the end of the day.

It was a great way to weed out the potential problems before the real thing. We all learned our lessons well.

We were told that there is no competition in foxhunting unless it's a competition in courtesy, to participate with safety, fun in mind, and always smile at all the landowners. Without them, there would be no hunt!

My biggest smile came when Dave told me that Sewz and I could do it together! Here are his thoughts of that day, that I suspect he may have passed on to a young stable mate over the fence the following morning.

The First Hunt

It was a day made for horses!
The air was cool and bright.
I knew that something was afoot;
She groomed me half the night!
We've practiced all the courses
And a promise I can keep, is
To take each jump she asks of me
I can do them in my sleep!

We trotted up to Hubbard's Hill
And what a sight I saw!
There were trailers, riders, horses,
Maybe forty head or more
There were men with whips and blowing horns
And a herd of matching dogs!
The excitement was contagious
We were all agog!

They were moving in a circle
All at once, not like a show.
They were getting set for something
But what, I didn't know!
They called us all together...
I could hardly catch my breath
My heart was pounding like a drum.
I was really scared to death!

Then something must have spooked the leader
A fright we didn't need!
He must have seen a Devil Beast
'Cause it started a stampede!
That Beast will bring down anyone
Who can't keep up, you see.
I put it right in overdrive
'Cause he never will catch me!

She tried so hard to rein me in. But
I didn't give a hoot!
We were running for our lives
With that Beast in hot pursuit!
And I knew that other dangers
Were hiding in the corn
It warned us with its whispering
As we all sped along.

But then a strange thing happened
Like I had done this all before
An overwhelming feeling
That was too strong to ignore
It was a thousand years ago
The pattern was so clear!
The predator! The herd in Flight!
That's what's happening here.

But I felt their strength around me!
Their power and their speed
And I'm with them! I'm one of them!
A member of this breed!
And so with all my panic as
We madly galloped on
In the midst of all my brothers,
My fears were slowly gone.

We galloped through the meadows!
We trotted through the woods
We crossed the streams, we jumped the logs
I was starting to feel good!
I thought no more about that Beast.
We were sort of having fun.
I think by then we'd lost him
When we made that downhill run.

Sometimes we forget our roots
As we're daily serving "them"

But if they take you on a hunt
You can be a horse again!
Trust me, you're gonna love it
And just to quell your fears
It's a run that we've been making
For a hundred thousand years!

It's our game, you see, that they all play
With a little different twist
Because they're flying with our herd
It's a thrill they can't resist!
Now I'll tell you the secret
So you'll know when you begin
The Beast is never chasing us,
But we've been chasing him!

Hunting was like being in a beautiful, moving oil painting. Every moment changed to another lovely scene. I loved it. My horse took to it like a duck to water once he caught on to what it was all about. He seemed to know when the season began each year and would put himself on a diet, leaving half of his grain every day. He would also stop eating and rush to his window when the geese went over. I think he thought it was the voice of the hounds. When the trailer came to pick him up, he eagerly walked out with me and quickly backed into his berth. He knew where we were going.

In the field, when Dave's arm went up to signal we were on our way, I'm sure he was watching and would start prancing in place while I was still talking to someone. "C'mon, they're leaving! Let's go!" he'd be thinking.

Sewz was never a great leader, but he sure was a great follower. He'd jump over a truck if he had a lead. He'd never lose sight of that tail in front of him, no matter how high the jump or how deep the ravine. I quickly realized all I needed to do was to put him in back of a dependable old hunter and it worked fine for us and we'd both have a terrific time.

One of my great thrills came when, after a few years, a friend who was always training big thoroughbred hunters asked if we'd be her lead. It was a compliment like someone had told me my kids were polite or smart or beautiful...the same kind of thrill.

Four years later, never having missed a Sunday hunt, we were awarded our colors at the ball that year. I felt like

Cinderella, everyone congratulating me and asking me to dance! Sewz, on the other hand, who had enabled us to accomplish it all, was snoozing in his stall, but the next morning was his! I had braided his mane with the colors of our hunt, and stayed up until 2 a.m. sewing mine on my collar. When we were asked to join the Master up front, Sewz was a little hesitant and couldn't believe I was allowing him to parade past all the others when I had been holding him back for so long, and from that day on we rode directly in back of the Master. He knew that was the safest place in the herd and he would never be held in back again.

When my daughter and I returned from a ride one evening, Dave told us that he had just taught his last lesson. He had decided that the barn would go back to just being his private barn and the boarders would have to find other accommodations.

I couldn't sleep that night. I was so saddened that our little barn family would all be scattered. The next few weeks everyone was talking about where they'd go and what they'd be doing. Some would go to other barns. Some talked of building or bringing their horses home. We all knew it was the end of an era and a big part of our lives was over. It would never be quite the same again.

My dream was to have my horse closer to me, not further away. I had always been able to ride my bike up to Dave's barn every day, it was so close. Our property wasn't big enough to put up a barn with pasture but we did have an oversized, attached garage! I mustered the courage to ask my husband if he really cared if the cars never saw shelter again. A great meal and a big hug usually renders him defenseless. He does realize that I'm much easier to live with when I'm happy and he knew my attachment to my horse. He okayed the idea!

My sadness about leaving the old barn waned while looking forward to setting up my own and taking on the complete care and feeding of my good friend. But he had to have a horse friend too and we asked Sally's owner if we could bring her with us. Unfortunately, she had other plans and would be sending her elsewhere for training. Our daughter was heartbroken. We half-heartedly started a search to find a friend for Sewz. Money and time was the issue. We had invested a lot in converting the garage into a barn. I call it the "barrage" now. We really didn't have time or money to look for the perfect horse to replace Sally. The deadline to leave the old barn was closing in on us. We decided this search was just for a friend for Sewz. We could afford an aged friend or an untrained youngster!

We vied for the youngster!

We found a ten month old, black colt with white pastern socks in back, a white stripe down his nose and attitude. He was full of spirit and personality and was brave to a point of recklessness! Nothing phased him. He bravely jumped into the trailer as though he had done it many times before, cutting quite a dashing figure in his little red shipping wraps and new lead and halter. I thought later how he must have felt before we found him.

Colt for Sale (for Shaddles)

I know I'm up for sale
And I'm waiting every day,
　　To see who looks me over
And hear just what they say.

　　The old gelding really scares me
With the stories that he tells
　　Of the other barns he's been
Where they don't treat you very well.

　　Where the hay is old and dusty
And the stalls are dark and bare,
　　And you never get to play outside
With other horses there.

　　Where sometimes they forget your grain
And the water's never clean
　　Where they use the whip for nothing
And the stablemen are mean!

　　I hope I can please someone
Who is kind and patient, too
　　Who explains to me exactly
What they're asking me to do.

　　I hope they never whip me
If I don't understand,

A little tap will show me
And I'll do what they command.

A little boy may be there
When I get to the new place
        With hair the shade of carrots
And freckles on his face.

Or a little girl may want me
With ribbons in her hair,
        Who'll make a picnic for us
In a meadow we can share.

Wait! I think I see a trailer
It's pulling in our yard!
        Wish I could see it better.
I'm trying very hard!

Uh oh! Here comes ole'jim
To put my halter on!
        A few last steps and in the rig!
In a moment we'll be gone!

I keep calling as we're leaving.
I can hear them answer, then...
        I can't help but wonder
If I'll see them all again...

This trailer ride seems endless,
And if we go too far
        I guess I'll never find my way
Back to the "Lucky Star"!

We're turning down a tree lined road
With fenced meadows everywhere.
        There's timothy and clover!
I can smell it in the air!

Look! There's someone tall and pretty!
I see her at the door
With an apple and a smile!
I'm not worried anymore!...

We called him Shadrach, and when he and Sewz were turned out together for the first time it wasn't a very friendly beginning. Sewz made it very clear who would be the boss and who would be the lacky. Sewz was really in great shape at the time and Shad had been overfed and under worked, so there was really no contest. The chase was on. After a dozen laps around the field, Shad stood in the corner puffing and submissively let Sewz sniff him out from stem to stern. The finale was when Sewz put his nose between Shad's back legs and virtually lifted his hind end off the ground with his head. It was the ultimate humiliation. Everyday for weeks when they were turned out, Sewz would immediately give Shad the "evil eye", and chase him around a bit to make sure he didn't forget the deal they had struck.

They did become best friends (after all, they only had each other) and would play stallion games and lip wrestle everyday. Sewz eventually made Shad the second in command.

Shadrach got his name from a bible story... one of the children thrown into the fiery furnace and saved by an angel of the Lord. The lady from whom we bought him had found a group of young horses who were being raised for meat and found homes for all of them. She was their angel. She took the personality kid home herself, but she had small children and was expecting another and so the ad went in the paper, and that's how we found him.

He was a most entertaining horse. When I would go out to ride and he was left alone he would always throw a little temper tantrum. He would paw the ground and rear and whinney, and while on his hind legs he would kick out with his back ones. (A cabriole? A little Lippizaner in his genes?) Then he would race in a circle. I don't know how long it continued as he'd still be doing it until I could no longer see him.

When we returned, he'd always call to us from a great distance. He couldn't see us coming and I wondered if it was our smell on the breeze or the vibrations of our hooves that he picked up through his hooves.

We had a fence with three horizontal wooden slats about 4'6" high. He was still quite small and would reach between the slats to the grass on the other side. He discovered if he put his weight on the middle slat, he could snap it and sort of stumble out into the great green beyond. He seemed to enjoy doing that and had no qualms about being out on his own and leaving the rest of the herd.

We live near a golf course and I could just envision him doing his little dance on the 9th hole, and the inevitable lawsuit! We finally covered the inside of the fence with mesh.

One morning I was getting ready to go to a luncheon and had just gotten out of the shower, wrapped a towel around me and stepped into my big fuzzy slippers. A glance out the window showed me that the escape artist had managed to break out of stir again, and was peacefully grazing near the practice polo field! I grabbed a cup of grain, a rope and a halter and flew out the door, not caring about how I was dressed. I just wanted to catch him before he went any further. No matter how I coaxed, I couldn't get that lead over his neck, and I was running late.

I used up all the grain and still he managed to avoid the halter. He was really laughing at me and I was becoming more and more enraged. I knew I was losing the argument. I turned away to run back to get more grain, having a few moments while he was in that knee deep new grass. That's when I realized there were others laughing at me, too. Not far from where I was, the DPW men were repairing the road and they had seen the whole episode.

I was so embarrassed! They were all hooting and hollering at me by then! Trying to ignore them and hide my embarrassment, I turned for home at least to get some clothes on. I had gone a few yards when I suddenly felt a presence in back of me... of course it was Shad. The fun was over, he'd had his fill and dutifully followed me right into the barn where he was quickly apprehended and locked up! I even made it in time for the luncheon.

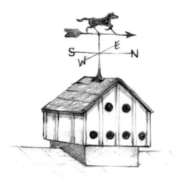

The accommodations in the barrage were proportionate to the Waldorf! We had built two twelve foot square box stalls, paneled the interiors with 3/4" heavy plywood and the dividers were 2" x 10"s, all painted white, bright and beautiful. Each stall had a window and we had four exposures, one side of which was never shut, according to the wind. We had hot and cold running water. We bedded in wood shavings. We had four feedings a day, except summer when they were out all day, daily turnout and carrots every night when I tucked them in and gave them a hug. No horse could want for more. I have spoiled them as I have my children.

We had a visitor two weeks after we moved in. It was Sally's owner's husband who had come to wish us luck with our new venture. I think we impressed him because we got a call the next day allowing Sally to come down to live with us. We were all thrilled and delighted. Our daughter rode her home from the other barn at 6 a.m. the following morning in time for breakfast! Now we had three.

Of course, we hadn't planned for three, but we put a 2" x 6" board across the other side of the barn to contain her and one for bedding on the bottom and she was contented and happy to be with Sewz again. One morning I woke up and found them both in her stall, side by side. Sewz has a magic lip and he had managed to open his door and jump into her stall. The 2" x 6" had remained in place. I will never figure out how he accomplished that feat! Sewz had a very smug look on his face.

Some of our other four legged friends did not fare as well. One, especially, was a little dappled buckskin who was born on Good Friday, and that was his name. His owners had gone to a house sale to buy a desk and brought him home, too. He had been at Dave's barn with all of us when we all made our move and he was brought home to a lovely little barn with a walk-in to his stall and a split rail fence around a nice paddock. It had a big tree in the middle, all his very own. But that was the problem. It was all his own, shared with no one. I would pass everyday, winter or summer, and he'd be standing next to his old tree in the middle of the field... I could feel his loneliness and it made me sad. His owners were gone all day and it was a very quiet place. I knew he needed a friend, a dog, a cat, a goat or even a chicken. His mistress laughed when I made the suggestion. I'm sure she thought I was a nut. But here are his thoughts in his loneliness.

Horse Alone (for Friday)

I'm so alone, where can there be
Another creature just like me?
The days are long and here I stand
Abandoned in a lonely land...

I don't remember how I strayed
Or did they leave? Was I afraid?
Did they lose me or I lose them?
I can't remember how or when...

The old tree is my only friend.
I stand beside it and pretend
I feel some warmth, not far apart,
The pounding of another heart.

I smell my brother. I hear the sound
Of stamping hooves upon the ground.
I see his breath through half closed eyes.
I feel my legs begin to rise!!

Again! Again! We're running now!

Everything is right somehow!
A friend! A friend! We're right in stride,
Twin shadows running side by side!

He looks like me! He smells like me!
A herd of two...what ecstasy!
How wonderful my life can be,
Another creature just like me!!

This is why I've yearned so much,
Another pair of eyes to watch
Another pair of ears to hear
Lest predators are stalking near!

I was half, now I am whole.
The need is filled within my soul.
I've waited for this moment when
I'd never be alone again...

But, suddenly I hear a sound...
My ears snap up. I look around
My head is still, my nostrils flare.
I see I've just been standing there.

I'm so alone, where can there be
Another creature, just like me?

This tale does have a happy ending. A good Penny turned
up the following year. That was her name, a young bay mare...
a herd of two!

Meanwhile, back at the ranch, we were all living the good life, everyone happy and contented. There's nothing like having the horses at home with us. I love getting their grain ready at feeding time and hearing them nickering, knowing I'm coming. I love doing the stalls, believe it or not. It's my therapy. I love not having to ride up to the old barn to see my horse, but instead being able to look in on him anytime, day or night, even in my pajamas.

I'll never have to shovel a path in the snow out to the barn when it's right here! We sleep in the tack room if someone's having a problem at night. We can hear every sound, when they shake their buckets or get up from sleep. Shad calls the alarm by raking his teeth on the mesh if someone gets out of their stall.

When people come to the house for the first time and see the horses peering out of the garage as they pull in the driveway, they all remark how quaint it is, like in England or

Europe, and I'm always flattered! You know the animal people by their comments. One day, a woman came to the house and she was definitely not an animal person. She moved away from the cat when he rubbed against her legs and sneered with disdain when the dog started barking. Her comment on the horses was, "But what do you do about the odor?" I off handedly said, "Oh, they don't mind our smell at all!"

We have other unwelcome guests at the barrage, and everywhere else, in the summer time, as a matter of fact. Flies! The curse of the horse. I can't think why the good Lord placed them on this earth with no valid use or reason except maybe to make winter more bearable. We fight them tooth and tail every summer.

We keep them out of the barn quite nicely but even with wipe, spray and fly masks they still bother the horses outside and it bothers me to see it. Hence this thought for all horses who wait, with patient resignation, to come in to get away from the pests for a nice afternoon siesta in the cool of the barn on a hot summer afternoon.

Summer Flies

I've been out here thirteen hours
And I know its in their power
To give me a little shower
And a rub!

I really have been fightin'
On my eyes and ears they're lightin'
Those darn flies just keep bitin'
Drawin' blood!

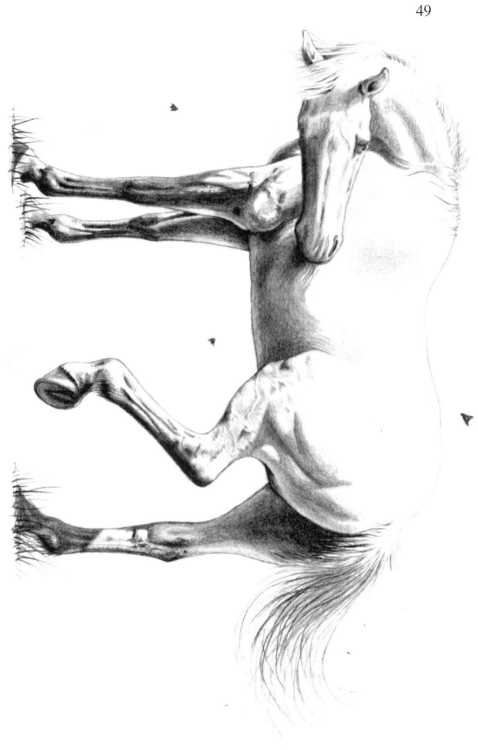

> If I could live my dream
> I'd be in a mountain stream
> With a waterfall to teem
> Upon my sides.
>
> There would stand a lovely mare
> With tail poised in the air
> To strike any fly who dares
> To touch my hide!
>
> But while my tail is swishin'
> I can only go on wishin'
> That they fill my sole ambition
> Right away!
>
> I keep sweatin' and keep kickin'
> And still the clock keeps tickin'
> Let's hear that gate latch click
> And make my day!

Sally went on her first hunt with our daughter that fall. Her owner had told us it would be a cold day in hell when we got that mare to hunt, but she did it and she was wonderfully quiet. I think she was in awe of it all. Everyone who knew her was congratulating our daughter and she was so happy to have (almost) her own hunter.

But the next hunt, Sally went crazy. All the old emotions kicked in and she became dangerous and foolish and had to be pulled off the field. It was a black day for Diana.

Half our family was foxhunting then, two sons, a

daughter in law, our daughter and myself. Another son flies a plane and my husband patiently puts up with us all.

Well, the search began for another horse to hunt as clearly Sal was never going to catch on to it, and a four horse herd sounded like a nice, even number. No one would ever have to stay home alone. We talked to everyone and answered all the ads in the paper and quickly found that it was just like going to the pound to find a new puppy or kitten. We wanted to take them all home and give them a good meal. Our daughter having been rescuing kittens, puppies, boys and now horses all her life, found a big black fellow with a star on his brow that you could always see when you looked in on at them night. She knew she could save him as well. She doesn't take after the pebbles in the street.

He needed a good deal of training as he was hardly aware of even basic groundwork. He was frightened of everything, even the gentlest touching. Some cruel treatment must have been in his background. I always hear a voice from somewhere inside a horse and his voice said, "don't hurt me..." We named him Starbuck and we had to introduce him to the herd. We were keeping them in our neighbors five acre field that summer, walking them home at night and had stabled the new one in that neighbor's barn, so we had some room for the meeting.

This is the tale of that day from the King of the Herd (Sewz) when we turned them loose together.

The Intruder

I was gazing across our field one day
When, what d'ya know to my dismay
    They let some stranger in to eat our grass!
He looked like a dark and sinister dude and,
    If he thought for a moment he could intrude,
He'd better know that we were gonna clash!

I went after him like a hawk in flight!
Thought I'd better set things right
    My ears flat back and my angry teeth were bared!
He saw me coming and he started to run.
    He knew his troubles had just begun.
And let me tell you, he was running scared!

The other two saw me and joined the chase!
We circled the field like a Derby race.
    And I have to admit that this guy had some speed,
But the stakes were high and his chances slim.
    We ran him in the corner and we boxed him in,
'Twas then he knew his doom was guaranteed!

There was a tangle of legs and manes and squeals
Of gnashing teeth and of flying heels!
    I turned my back to send him to the moon!
The others gave him some nips and lumps.
    My two back hooves tattooed his rump!
My trademark won't be fading very soon!

Well, we were all puffin' and pretty beat,
And there was sun to enjoy and grass to eat.
    So after one more round we walked away to graze,
But we kept watching him with threatening eyes,
    To let him know that if he were wise,
He'll remember these lessons all his living days!

You don't barge in if no one's asked ya'.

After all, it's not your pasture.
My word is law 'round here 'cause I'm the boss.
If you want to share then ya' gotta earn it.
Give us respect and we'll return it,
And keep the ancient ethic of the horse.

Well, some time has passed since that troublesome day,
But he's behaved himself and learned our ways.
And through it all there really is a plus,
If they pull that stupid trick again
And let another new horse in,
The big black stranger, now, is one of us.

Diana rode Starbuck in an arena when she first bought him and he seemed to be a little too unpredictable to figure out. His fear of any change of leg, weight or rein, and his unexpected reactions seemed odd. She decided to hire a trainer to work with him with very unsatisfactory results. He seemed to become more and more nervous and less and less trusting. She then decided to ask a knowledgeable friend, familiar with training difficult horses, to see what she could do.

She chose to long line him first. Getting his bridle on was difficult enough, but when she tried to move him forward standing in back of him he became panicked and belligerent. He spun around over Diana, who was leading him, and started striking at the "trainer" with his front hooves. One of the long lines caught under his tail. Diana rushed over to dislodge it as he was completely berserk by then.

Our friend is a short lady and the horse a massive black blur above her, plus, she had tripped and fallen in the ditch at the side of the road. We thought it was her end. She was laughing it off and saying it was fine, not to worry. Through all of this she had never let go of the lines, and her plan was to drive him down the road and back. She was determined to do it. She depended greatly on her voice that she used with upward inflections like a little "whoop" when she said "good" or "good boy". Miraculously she got him moving forward and we watched in awe as she drove him down the road and the little whoops became less audible. As she disappeared over the hill we looked at each other as if to say, "My God, I think she's got it."

Diana and I sat down and waited for them to reappear. As they rounded the top of the knoll, everything seemed in control, but when Starbuck knew he was heading home, he started to move faster. The driver was running as fast as her little legs could carry her and she went down when Starbuck left the road to join Diana and I in the field, dragging her the rest of the way. He stopped next to us and put his nose under Diana's arm for protection.

Out of breath and laughing, she said, "We'll try in the paddock next time instead of the open road." Diana and I really thought she was a hound for punishment and should have resigned this commission at this point, but we said she was welcome to try again the following week.

Starbuck had severe allergies and we knew we had to do any work with him before the black flies arrived in our area which kicked off the allergies. Well, she couldn't come the following week but came the next one. She managed only to mount up before the flies moved in and it was over! Starbuck ran blindly forward through the fence with rider on the ground, having been catapulted off of him the moment she put her weight on his back. The rein somehow looped over the post, catching him or he would have been in the next county before we caught up with him.

This was the end of Starbuck's training. We found out a lot through the years about Starbuck's history, the most important fact being that he had been in a training program at a local agricultural college and had been labeled "incorrigible" and drummed out of the corps. What cruel and inhumane treatment had befallen him beforehand? I think someone tried to train him with a cattle prod as the first fly sting of the season virtually sends him into hysteria.

He has very low self-esteem and spends most of his life making believe he is invisible. If there is an argument in the herd, he never becomes involved and stands quietly at a distance. Diana says he'll buy a drink for the winner, whoever it is. There is a lot to be said about a good companion horse who never causes anyone any problems. If anyone needs a friend, he is there for them as he knows what it's like to be ragged on and can commiserate with them. He's fine with grooming now, with the vet and with the farrier, but we know better than to try to ride or work him again.

Well, we couldn't stand his hysterical screaming when we'd put him in the neighbor's barn and brought the others home to the barrage at night. It didn't seem fair, so, you guessed it, he's here too. He's happy, we're happy and he's a beautiful black satin reflection midst the green grass and daisies to admire in the field.

Sometimes I'd miss seeing our friends at the old barn, as much the horses as the people. One horse in particular was a special favorite because he was my horse's best friend. They had been turned out together everyday. Our son was taking care of him and riding him at that time as his owner was out of town a lot. He is a big lumbering bay of dubious heritage although he has the look of a Cleveland Bay. He has wonderful golden eyes and a sweet expression and in spite of his size is gentle as a lamb. His name is Fox.

When Fox and Sewz were turned out together it was sheer poetry in motion. The minute they were in the field, the show was on! They'd run as fast as they could, together like fish in a pond, making the same moves at the same instant, taking the jumps as pairs, then separating and circling the field in the opposite direction. When they met at the other side, confronting each other, they would rear up on their hind legs, then run as pairs again. This went on for at least ten minutes before they would settle down to graze. It was such a predictable show that people would come out to watch, and say, "Gee, I wish my horse would do that! He just stands and does nothing when I put him out." I felt my horse and I were blessed with such a good friend.

I knew that Fox and Sewz would always be best friends because their first meeting and time together was so idyllic. My friend invited us on a picnic! All we had to do was join them. I wondered how we'd pull this off on horses but I thought we'd give it a try... she'd be riding Fox and would bring everything. When she suggested putting the leads and halters on to let them graze, I wasn't going to let go of that lead! I wondered how I would manage the lemonade, strawberry shortcake and my horse all at the same time!

We were in the middle of a lovely meadow and I noticed how mellow the two horses were munching side by side, as though they'd known each other for years. I quietly put down the lead and sat down a short distance away and enjoyed a great lunch. I know now how foolish it was, but you have to remember I was very new to the game at that time and never gave it any thought that they really could have taken off for home at any time. We could have been left to carry saddles, bridles and picnic baskets about five miles on foot... not to mention the danger to the horses crossing the roads.

The fates were kind to us and as the sun began to lower, we packed up for the ride home. The horses became soul mates!

Everyday, when I went up to ride, I walked in and called out, "Here I am," and Sewz and Fox would nicker in unison! They knew they'd each get a carrot and would finish up with a run together out in the pasture and some grazing time.

Well, after a couple of months, I decided to visit our old friend at his new barn. When I walked in, I called out, "Well, here I am!" His beautiful low nicker gave me goose bumps. He remembered me! He took the carrot and turned away, not like him to do that. He usually would wait for a face rub. I sadly realized he still had the saddle mark on his back from the last hunt the month before. These must have been his thoughts at that time.

The Neglected Horse (for Fox)

The dawning of another day....
Will this be the one? The day I'm set free?
Every day I wait expectantly but no one comes...
another sunrise another sunset.
My stall has become my prison.
I watch with envy the others with their human friends.
They're allso happy. My legs are so stiff. I yearn to run again.
Will I ever feel the earth fly beneath my hooves.... to race

the meadow with a friend? Ah, the meadow, how wonderful to graze, to roll, to scratch my back on an old tree. I itch.

I envy the barn dog. I watch him scratch. It looks so good. I can almost feel his delight when he hits the right spot. If only God gave me toenails or humans more compassion.

Why am I being punished like this? What did I do wrong?

My hooves need trimming. My mane covers my eyes. My coat is dull. I need grooming so badly.

If they lock us up like this and take us from the herd, we need a human friend!

I remember I had one once. We went out everyday and we worked hard but he always told me I had done well and gave me a carrot and a shower if I was sweaty... and I always felt good.

He'd brush me and talk to me and get all the pebbles out of my hooves every day. I slept good at night and I was happy. I knew he cared.

The world is filled with happiness, but not for me.

Now I stare out of my window at night and think of those days...how good they were, good memories make the time bearable. I have fresh water and good hay and a clean stall. They pay for that. But I need someone who cares. Indifference is a cruel fate. When will they remember? I'm a person too. Happiness abounds but not for me.

A few months later Fox's owner left the area and I was elated to hear he had been given to a lady who rode every day and gave him a lot of TLC. He surely deserved it after a siege of neglect. In fact, he is thirty-two years old now and he hunted again this year. He is certainly made of the right stuff.

There are so many tales to tell, but I try to narrow down to the ones that touch my heart or tickle my funny bone. This one did the former.

I was up very late one night working on one of my sewing deadlines. When I finally turned out the lights it was close to 2:30 a.m. I glanced out the window and saw that Sewz was still awake and gazing out into the night. The stars were just dazzling, right down to the horizon. I couldn't resist going out to talk to him, but he never broke his intent gaze as I put my arm up under his neck to rub his cheek on the other side, looking in the same direction, "What are you looking at? What do you see out there, Sewz?" We were both staring at the cloudless sky.

Suddenly there was a bright swish of a shooting star across the entire sky. I had never seen a shooting star like that before. It was just spectacular!

When it burned out of sight, Sewz sighed deeply, left his window and went back to the corner of his stall to rest. I think he knew it was coming! I think he waited for it, and I'm so happy I happened in on his rendezvous with that star.

Sewz and I share the same birthday. Maybe there's something astrological about our relationship!

And this one is for your funny bone.

I rode up to "dead goat" hill one day. The name hardly describes the beauty of the place! It's the highest point in our area and the view of the lake and hills and the surrounding countryside is exquisite. It's the sort of spot when you're out on your horse alone that makes you thank the good Lord for giving it all to you to enjoy. Of course, in my stopping to drink in all the beauty, my horse gets a chance to gobble up a bit of alfalfa on the edge of the farmers' fields. His thanks must be for my letting him do that!

While watching the bees, busy at work in the alfalfa blossoms, I realized that shadows were passing over me, like an airplane shadow passing between me and the sun. When I looked up, I was shocked to see five huge birds circling above me! They looked pretty darned ominous and sure had ideas about us!

Sewz got the message too and we high-tailed it back down the hill and into the woods for some cover! I kept thinking of those monstrous birds all the way home and couldn't wait to tell my husband my latest adventure. I excitedly told the story as he patiently listened to me with a little smile on his face. Then he said with such sincerity, "Why, Juann, they were horse hawks and about to carry you off!" My dropped jaw and wide eyed reaction made him burst into laughter. I've always been a gullible fool around that man!

A week or so later, a neighbor stopped me on the road and asked if I had seen anything of the turkey buzzards that had been sighted in this area. They usually don't get this far north.

Well, if I ever see them again, I'll always call them horse hawks.

I was invited to go to a hunter pace down at Cornell University with three other ladies and their horses. My partner would be a dear friend, Gayle, and her trusty mount, Dudley... she with her twenty-two year old horse, and I with mine. I felt a deep connection with Gayle and Dudley because their partnership was so similar to ours. Neither partner held more stock in the company than the other. It was a 50/50 relationship. If they both weren't having a good time, there was no deal. I guess you could say we both rode with the same wild abandon, but both horses knew exactly what they were doing and took good care of their riders.

There were over one hundred and fifty participants that day and all four of us came within seconds of optimum time! It was cool and breezy, and the tailgate picnics were everywhere. Our table was especially festive as it was Gayle's birthday and we had a wonderful lunch topped off with birthday cake and champagne.... a grand memory to treasure.

A few months later Gayle stopped over to bring good news, and bad. The good news was that I was invited to a baby shower! Mimi, one of the other ladies at the pace, had just announced the arrival of a little foal... the bad news was that Gayle had to put Dudley down. He had been slowly going blind and had become dangerous to himself. Her words hit me like a blow to the solar plexus. We cried a bit with feelings only one horse person to another can feel. She was so devastated she said she didn't think she'd ever have another horse, the hurt was too much. I was sure there would be another horse in her future, but I couldn't even think of that for her now. I knew there was nothing I could do or say to help mend her broken heart or make her feel any better, but I knew someone who could. Dudley.

These are his words to her.

On Parting (to Gayle from Dudley)

The world grew dark, then disappeared
And for a moment I was gone,
But now I'm here in paradise
I'm young and well as if reborn!

The sky is clear, the air is sweet,
Green pastures spread beneath my feet
My soul is happy here, it's true
But my spirit and my heart's with you

Between us there's a special bond
That stretches ever far beyond
All worldly ties that we have ever known
Trusting partners all the time
My life in your care, yours in mine
The faith and loyalty we both have shown

So when you're standing at the barn
A velvet nose will touch your arm
And there is no one there that you can see
It will be me....

When the autumn geese appear
A distant, haunting call you'll hear
And it will make you smile so tenderly
It will be me...

Some night when you're in your bed
We're flying through the woods ahead
And you will think "He's gone, how can this be?"
But we can never be apart
Because we're in each other's heart
And you will come to know
It will be me...

Now, somewhere as the days go by,
They'll bring a horse for you to try
And you'll observe him so reluctantly
But deep inside his eyes so dark
You'll find a reminiscent spark that
Tugs your heartstrings unmistakenly
It could be me...

Well, Gayle has been riding a friend's sweet, little mare for a couple of years now. I think she sees the spark in her and is thinking of making an offer on her someday. I just love happy endings... or new beginnings.

Gayle's terrible loss made me realize what a traumatic

experience she had suffered... like losing a child, so helpless and dependent.

I thought of all the wonderful times my horse and I have shared together. I don't think there is any sport where you are so much a part of nature, riding trails, becoming one with your horse and experiencing the same joy and exhilaration in the wild, unspoiled part of the countryside. I always thought it was a little miracle that an animal as ponderous as a horse would allow a person to get on its back and take them wherever they'd like to go!

Well, we've run with the deer, we've flown with the geese and we sing with the birds (he's a great alto). Every ride is better than the last one.

One time, it had been raining heavily for three days and I was getting restless to get out on the trails again. I woke up to a gloomy day, totally overcast, but at least no rain. I put on my rain gear, just in case, and started out.

We went deep into the woods that day exploring where we had never been before. We have a lot of thickets, low growth and wetlands that I try to avoid, but this day I found I was deeper into that area than I really wanted to be. I had been out longer than usual and it was getting late. I realized that to avoid the bog, I had to get through the thickets. I had no idea how I got where I was as there really wasn't much of a path.

There were no telephone poles or any sunlight to guide me. I was really lost! I thought of my husband always telling me to bring the cell phone and did I have my watch. Of course, even if I could call, where would I tell him I was? How could I call him to come pick me up? I'd never take either as I felt that one or the other would inhibit my freedom in some way. I'd rather be lost to the world... but let me say, not this lost! I did feel a little moment of panic, but I remembered a story a friend had told me.

He'd been camping in the High Sierras and in taking a shortcut back to camp, found himself in the middle of an impassible area of trees collapsed into a steep ravine that went on for miles making it impossible to continue on horseback. He was alone with a horse he called a "dim bulb" in whom he had little confidence. He thought the only way he or the horse had a chance was to get off, untack him, turn him lose, and hope they could both find their way back.

He carried his tack until he was able to get out of the abyss, about three hours. Exhausted, he fell asleep and woke up at daybreak to finish the trek back to camp. Tired and hungry he finally spotted the camp in the distance and who was peacefully munching grass next to it but that ole "dim bulb"! How remarkable these creatures are!

In my predicament, I asked Sewz if I were a wounded

Indian, could he get me back to my tepee? I leaned forward and rested the side of my head on his neck and mane and relaxed my hold on his reins. He questioned my relaxing in the saddle, going one way then the other. Was I leaving the decision to him? My eyes were closed (don't forget I'm wounded). He'd go forward, then back a little, then turn, then forward again, avoiding the vines and thickets. After a while, the pace quickened, but I didn't sit up yet. He made another turn and started to trot. I knew he had found a viable path to continue. Then I sat up, but never picked up the reins. He had me back on the familiar trail in five minutes! You know they say there is no perfect horse, but there is because I own him... or he owns me. I don't know which, but all who know us are aware of his opinion on the subject.

I am as happy as he is when I can turn him out in a dandelion field on a sunny summer morning!

DANDELION FIELD

I plunge into the golden sea
And bathe myself in luxury.
My hooves are dancing on the sky
No horse can be as bless'd as I
I must have found that pot of gold
At rainbow's end, so I've been told
I rub my back in the sweet doubloons
My life's so good, the world's in tune!

But now I'd better cease the dance
Don't want to miss my only chance
    To gather each coin, one by one
Continue 'til the day is done
    And when she calls, and I must depart
I'll head home with a happy heart
    To spend the night in sweet repose
With my pot of gold and a yellow nose!

Winters are pretty rigorous where we live and I find myself waiting for the first sign of spring like a child waiting for her birthday, counting the days on the calendar. I make the first entry each year on the fifteenth of April. It says, "grass is growing." And I keep telling the boys, "Don't worry, it's coming... pretty soon now." I like to think they understand, if not, it makes me feel better anyway.

A flock of geese flew over this morning heading home to Canada in a blinding snowstorm, six to eight inches of lake effect! They must know something we don't know!

The geese are the harbingers of spring and fall in our area. We live in the fly way of the Canadian geese and they take rest stops on our beautiful lake. At the first sound of their voices when winter has started to fade, we all run out to watch them pass in their beautiful formations to wish them a safe trip home. They are truly on the cutting edge of the season.

How do you suppose they pick their leaders, the broadest wingspan or the best navigational expertise or the loudest "HONK" ? Or does the one with the least patience, that can't stand waiting around another minute, take off first and the others blindly follow hoping he knows where he's going? Well, they've been traveling over us for a while now and even though there's still snow on the ground, the boys came in tonight with onions on their breath. They must have dug in the snow to get the wild onions as they are the first sign of green we have. When other forage is available they eat around the onions, but after six months with no fresh chlorophyll, even the onions taste good to them.

There are other signs of spring even though we can't see it yet. The house cat wants to go outside, the dog has made his first trip down to the village again and when I kissed my horse good morning, his hair stuck to my lips. What do the horses think of at this time of year? Are they counting the days like we are, or maybe this....

Dear Sweet Summer

When the cobwebs turn to crystal,
And the roof nails turn to stars,
There's magic every morning
In this little barn of ours...
Old Man Winter's outside blowing up
An icy, bitter storm,
But even with the snow out there,
In here it's cozy warm...

Now how can it be warm in here
When it's so cold outside?
It's because my Dear Sweet Summer
Picked this sheltered place to hide!

Way back in November, on a
freezing, rainy night
Flying with the autumn leaves and
In the fading light
She floated in the window
Although I don't know how
With all her wondrous powers
She settled in the mow.

I know she's in here hiding
From all the snow and rain
'Cause a field of dandelions' painted
On my window pane...
And also, every evening, much to
My delight,

I feel her lovely sunshine when
My blanket's on at night...

But when they bring my hay to me,
It's the nicest time of all,
When the smell of Dear Sweet
Summer surrounds me in my stall.
I push my muzzle in the hay
And toss it to the side
To find the clover blossoms
That summer's sun has dried.

Now winter holds her captive
While he plans his cold attacks
And taunts her when he pokes
His snowy fingers through the cracks!
So spring must pay her ransom
With one last icy gale
But he'll have no time to revel
As he's growing weak and frail.

And little spring grows stronger
With every lengthening day.
She'll cover him with blossoms
And cast his spell away.
Then they'll fling the barn doors open
And spring will set her free,
To make it warm and green for all
But especially for me.

And so to a new beginning..... Can't wait to get into the woods! Can't wait to gallop the fields! Can't wait to give Sewz a bath! Can't wait to get going again with my very own horse!

I hope all your childhood dreams come true as mine have. Make it happen by the time we meet again!

START EARLY!